MEMORY POCKETBOOK

By Vicki Culpin

Drawings by Phil Hailstone

"An elephant-like memory is no longer the preserve of the genius thanks to this book, which has over 14 years of expertise crammed into your back pocket. Use these tools to unlock your potential and retrieve what's on the tip of your tongue."
Lesley Richardson, Reporter, Press Association.

D1579287

Published by:
Management Pocketbooks Ltd
Laurel House, Station Approach, Alresford, Hants SO24 9JH. U.K.
Tel: +44 (0)1962 735573. Fax: +44 (0)1962 733637
E-mail: sales@pocketbook.co.uk
Website: www.pocketbook.co.uk

This edition published 2010

© Vicki Culpin 2010

British Library Cataloguing-in-Publication Data – A catalogue record for this book is available
from the British Library.

ISBN 978 1 903776 96 4

Design, typesetting and graphics by **efex ltd**. Printed in U.K.

CONTENTS

MYTHS & REALITY

INTRODUCTION

So, do you think you have a bad memory? Do you forget the times or locations of meetings, the names of new (or perhaps not so new!) colleagues or the key points for a presentation, in fact anything you haven't written down? Perhaps you don't completely forget information but just have a 'senior' moment – turn up for a meeting at the right time but the wrong place, call a colleague the wrong name or mislay a vital document you had 'just a minute ago'.

There are a number of reasons why, in a business environment, memory performance is likely to suffer. Perhaps surprisingly, none of these is likely to be age-related though stress, memory overload and lack of sleep can often be culprits.

This book will introduce you to the reasons you may suffer from poor memory performance at work, and how memory operates (which will help you understand how and why it fails and what you can do about this), along with providing some strategies to help you improve your memory in a variety of business situations and with a range of materials.

INTRODUCTION

Throughout the book you will also find sections entitled 'Not Convinced?' where we provide practical examples or demonstrations of the ideas and concepts under discussion. Feel free to skip over these exercises, but if you need convincing or want some practice, have a go. You may surprise yourself!

While the strategies included within this book will help you to improve your memory performance in a number of specific workplace scenarios, understanding the fundamentals of how memory works will also enable you to develop your own strategies and techniques – methods that work for you, in your own individual circumstances and organisational context.

A point worth noting at this stage: there is very little relationship between perceived memory ability and actual memory ability, so even if you think you have a poor memory there is hope!

MEMORY MYTHS

TRUE
FALSE

Memory: how it works, how to improve memory function and what happens when memory fails has been the topic of research for the medical profession, psychologists and other scientists for over two hundred years.

Along with a greater understanding of memory, the last two centuries have also established in the public mind a number of popular memory myths such as:

| Memory always gets worse as we age | Memory works like a muscle | It is possible to train your memory never to forget | The best way to remember anything is to create a visual image | Forgetting is not desirable, it is memory failure |

MEMORY REALITY

 Myth – Memory always gets worse as we age

Unfortunately, like all parts of the body, the brain deteriorates with age. A decline in memory performance with age is not inevitable, however, and is dependent on a large number of other factors, including the material you wish to remember and whether you have used a memory strategy.

Small changes in memory performance related to age are often blown out of proportion, with individuals becoming hyper-sensitive to forgetting and blaming age for every lapse or slip. If this describes you reflect back to your youth. Are you really much more forgetful now or do you just worry about your memory more? Are you busier now than when you were younger? Do you try to juggle more tasks at the same time? Are you more tired and do you take less exercise now? All of these behaviours affect memory just as much, if not more, than age *per se*.

MEMORY REALITY

Myth – Memory always gets worse as we age

Continued …

A study tracked 6,000 healthy adults over the age of 60 for a 10-year period and found that 70% of them showed no significant decline in memory ability.

Even if there are age-related changes in memory, they generally only become significant in healthy individuals over the age of 70 – usually beyond the age of retirement, so age cannot be used as an excuse for poor memory at work!

08967 244778
08842 479066
08267 882658
08543 207643
08732 449016
08936 372196
08433 556108
08673 741149
08983 903561

MEMORY REALITY

 Myth – Memory works like a muscle

The metaphor of a muscle is often used to explain how the brain works, so the assumption is that memory performance can be improved simply by exercising the brain through practice.

Research shows that long-lasting memory improvement is not achieved by simply practising memorising material (ie rote repetition). The true benefit of practice will only occur if it involves using a memory strategy or technique. We look at several different memory techniques later in the book.

MEMORY REALITY

Myth – It is possible to train your memory never to forget

It is inevitable that you will forget some information, and that other material will remain with you for a lifetime (the result of a well-practised technique or because the material is particularly strong, powerful or meaningful).

However, it is important to remember that all information (whether that be facts and figures from reports, people you meet during networking events or the key points for an upcoming presentation) is subject to the same laws of forgetting. While there are some things you may never forget owing to the strength of the memory trace (eg your first important presentation) or the number of times the memory is revisited (eg the time you made a serious mistake or error of judgement at work), it is not *impossible* for this memory to be forgotten.

MEMORY REALITY

 Myth – The best way to remember anything is to create a visual image

Some memory techniques and strategies are based around the principle that the best way to remember *any* type of information is to create a visual image of the material. While this may be an appropriate approach for certain types of information (eg complex diagrams), it is important to realise that factors such as type of memory, type of material and your preferred learning style all determine the most effective strategy for you.

Your memory is individual to you, and so the most effective ways to improve your memory will also be individual to you – there is no 'one size fits all'; no best way.

MEMORY REALITY

 Myth – Forgetting is not desirable, it is memory failure

If you feel you have a poor memory you will probably believe that forgetting is a weakness. While forgetting important material is obviously not ideal, we cannot and do not remember everything we perceive. If we could store and be able to recall everything we see, hear, smell, touch and taste in the world around us on a daily basis, the brain would be a very inefficient (and very cluttered) system.

The importance of the ability to forget can be demonstrated by the famous Russian mnemonist, V.S. Shereshevskii, known as S. S had an exceptional memory but found it virtually impossible to forget any information, no matter how mundane or boring. He ended his life in a Soviet asylum for the mentally ill. (See page 122 for more on S's extraordinary memory.)

Forgetting is an excellent evolutionary strategy for allowing you to function in the fast and ever faster business world. The key is to make sure you only forget what you don't need to remember!

CAUSES OF POOR MEMORY

MEMORY & STRESS

Do you ever find yourself forgetting even the most basic pieces of information during a really bad period of time at work?

Do you ever get home after a particularly stressful day in the office and, as you start to unwind, suddenly realise with horror that you have forgotten to do something quite important during the day?

Stress is one of the most common causes of poor memory performance. Stressful situations lasting weeks or months (whether the stress is work-related or personal) have been shown to impair communication between the cells in the regions of the brain responsible for learning and memory, particularly the hippocampus.

MEMORY & STRESS

When the body is experiencing a stressful situation, real or perceived, the adrenal glands secrete adrenalin, the 'fight or flight' hormone. If the perceived threat is still present after more than a few minutes, the body then secretes cortisol, the stress hormone. Cortisol diverts blood glucose (energy) to exercising muscles, to allow you to fight or run away. The amount of energy reaching the memory centres of the brain is much less than is needed to effectively create new memories or access existing ones. It had previously been thought that only chronic (long-term) stress reduces memory performance, but new research shows that after **only four days** of stresses cortisol leads to memory impairment.

There are, however, two pieces of good news. The first is that after one week without excess cortisol your memory performance will return to normal. The second is that after a very short, sharp stressor lasting no more than 20–30 minutes, short-term memory performance can actually increase.

Does *your* memory performance get worse when you are stressed? Reducing your stress levels will in turn reduce the cortisol in your blood. Along with giving huge health benefits, this may also help improve your memory.

MEMORY & SLEEP

Sleep is the next culprit when it comes to poor memory performance. After a bad night's sleep, how do you feel at work the next day? How about after several nights of disrupted sleep or if you are suffering from jet lag?

Common workplace complaints from individuals who have slept badly for one or two nights include headaches, blurred vision, emotionality (being either quick to anger or to cry), difficulty concentrating and lack of enthusiasm, to name but a few. All of these behaviours are clearly counterproductive in the workplace. But what about the relationship between sleep and memory? Does it just feel as though you cannot remember anything after a bad night's sleep or is memory really affected?

Research has found that going without sleep for 24 hours can lead to changes in behaviour equivalent to having drunk four glasses of wine – yes, four glasses of wine! How good is your memory after four glasses of wine?

MEMORY & SLEEP

While sleep research is really still in its infancy, it has been known for a number of years that sleep is very important for memory consolidation – that is, the brain's method of transferring new material and information to long-term memory (LTM). This transfer of information is from the hippocampus (where material is stored temporally and not particularly effectively) to the neocortex (where long-term memories are efficiently stored). Very recent studies have discovered that this transfer occurs through 'sharp wave ripples' which occur during deep sleep. So napping, while having other benefits, is not sufficient for memory consolidation.

Deep sleep appears to be the key, not just to retention or storage of information (consolidation), but also to retrieval (remembering), as sleep is thought to strengthen relevant associations between memories and weaken irrelevant associations.

So, how often do you sleep well, in terms of both quality (few awakenings) and quantity (adequate length)? What impact is this having on your ability to store and remember information?

MEMORY & MULTI-TASKING

In a busy work environment it is often second nature to multi-task – to check emails while on the phone or to read your Blackberry while in a meeting. In the hectic workplace typical of a 21st century organisation, multi-tasking is expected, and you probably often do it without even being aware of it.

Recent MRI (brain imaging) studies have shown that the brain is a lot less efficient at multi-tasking than we like to believe. The brain, while trying to do two things at once, actually switches tasks rather than conducting both simultaneously. Brain scans show that the areas of the brain responsible for the two tasks light up in turn rather than together – the brain switches off one task, albeit briefly, to concentrate on the other, and then shuts down the new area to revert to the original one.

A consequence of this task-switching may be poor memory. Research has shown that individuals who learn something new while multi-tasking are less able to recall what they have learned at a later date. Multi-tasking doesn't appear to impair the learning of information, but does make it much more difficult to remember it (and what good is learning if we cannot remember it?).

MEMORY & MULTI-TASKING

During multi-tasking we appear to code both the memory we hope to retain and the distracting information (a radio programme we were listening to or an email we were quickly checking). The memory and the distraction become entwined in our memory and the distractor becomes a cue to recall – we seem to be unable to remember the information without recalling the distractor first. This is related to the importance of context (see also the Cognitive Interview section later). How likely is it that, when trying to recall the key content of a phone call, you can actually remember the radio programme you had on at the time (you may not even have been aware you were listening)?

Multi-tasking reduces your ability to attend to the information you wish to learn. Ultimately we only have a finite resource of 100% attention. Doing two tasks together gives a maximum of 50% attention to each (we may like to think we can give 100% to both, but the scanning studies show this is not possible).

In the next few sections we look at the importance of attention in memory. The key point, though, is that **to ensure a strong and lasting memory, you need to give 100% attention.**

MEMORY & MULTI-TASKING

 Did you know that London Taxi Drivers who have completed 'the knowledge' (remembered all of the streets in the City of London) have enlarged hippocampi (the area of the brain responsible for learning and memory)?

 Did you know that birds with a bigger hippocampus have a longer lasting memory for where they stored their food compared with birds that have a smaller hippocampus?

STRUCTURE & TYPES OF MEMORY

TYPES OF MEMORY

Researchers often divide memory into different types, each with different characteristics. At present there is no model that successfully explains the entirety of memory function, but for the purposes of this book it is helpful for you to understand the distinction between two types of memory: **Short-Term Memory (STM) and Long-Term Memory (LTM)**.

Think about information that you only remember for a very short amount of time (eg a phone number that you need to write down). Now think about information that you can remember for a significant length of time (eg your first ever job interview).

The first piece of information will be stored briefly in STM while the second will be in LTM. In a business environment we rely on both STM and LTM to work effectively, eg you are sent an email with the time, date and agenda for a meeting next week. You read the email, and then delete it. In the next few seconds you write the time and location in your diary, using STM. During the meeting you recall the information necessary to discuss the agenda items, using LTM.

SHORT-TERM MEMORY

- How much information can you store in your STM?
- How long do you think information in your STM should last?
- How much information can you store in your LTM?
- How long do you think information in your LTM should last?

A famous experiment was conducted in 1956 by a psychologist called George Miller. He found that healthy adults could remember between five and nine single pieces of information (digits, letters or words) in STM, with an average of seven items.

SHORT-TERM MEMORY
NEED CONVINCING?

TASK

Cut a piece of A4 paper into nine separate squares and on each square write a digit from 1-9. Shuffle the pieces of paper and place them face down in front of you.

1	2	3
4	5	6
7	8	9

Turn each square over one at a time, at a rate of one per second, placing each new one on top of the preceding one. The task is for you to remember as many of the nine digits as you can, **in the order that you see them**.

When you have turned over all nine squares, write down, on a blank piece of paper, as many of the digits as you can remember, in the order that you saw them. Use a ? for any digits you cannot remember (eg 175?98??0).

Once you have completed the task, score yourself one point for each digit remembered in the correct place. This number is known as your STM digit span; that is the number of single digits you can remember, in order, in STM.

SHORT-TERM MEMORY

For many years psychologists believed that the amount we could hold in STM was determined by how many single pieces of information could be remembered; approximately seven.

Seven 'Pots'

More recent research has found, however, that we do not necessarily have a capacity of seven items; instead how much we remember in STM is partly determined by time. Instead of considering STM as the equivalent of having an average of 7 'pots' where pieces of information can be stored, it is now seen as a 'tape loop', with research finding that the length of the tape lasts between 2 seconds and 30 seconds, with an average of 15 seconds.

15 sec

'Tape Loop'

SHORT-TERM MEMORY

How much we remember in STM is, therefore, directly related to how much information (how many digits, words, letters or names of colleagues, etc) you can 'squeeze' into the tape loop in the approx 15 seconds of time you have, and how quickly you recall the information (eg how quick you are to write it down).

The more information you can squeeze into the 15 seconds and the faster you can output the information you have stored, the more you can remember in STM, so the better your STM will be. This concept will be examined further in the section on Improving STM.

LONG-TERM MEMORY

If STM is thought to be anything we can retain for a maximum of 30 seconds without any form of rehearsal, then LTM relates to any memory that we can remember for longer than, say, one minute.

Unlike STM, research on LTM has consistently shown that we can store large amounts of information in LTM for a very long period of time. That does not mean that LTM is infinite, however; just that the volume of memories created within your life span is less than that which you can store.

We must also be aware that even if a memory is stored, we still may not be able to access it; successful memory depends upon both effective **storage** and effective **retrieval**. Both storage and retrieval strategies will be discussed later.

TYPES OF LONG-TERM MEMORY

Think about every aspect of your business life and write a list of as many different types of material as you can think of that you need to store in your LTM. Once you have created the list, review it. Is there any way you can group the items within the list? Do certain types of material share characteristics? Your list could be: phone numbers, email addresses, where files are stored on the computer, access code to the front door, credit card pin number, how to get voicemail messages from phone, latest budget figures, appointment on Monday, information for next appraisal interview, names of the two new administrative assistants, etc.

The list you have created may contain 30 or 40 items (if it only contains one or two, see if you can subdivide further – eg if you have listed 'meetings' what is it about meetings that you need to retain; names, minutes, action points etc). You could group them according to the decade in which they were experienced, the emotionality of the memory, the type (eg faces, finances, department you worked in) or whether the memory was personal to you or external to you.

TYPES OF LONG-TERM MEMORY

Researchers have found that LTM can be subdivided into a number of different types, with each type having different characteristics. Three basic ways of subdividing LTM are:

- Episodic memory
- Semantic memory
- Procedural memory

Both episodic memory and semantic memory are key to successful performance in a business environment, whereas procedural memory (which is concerned with remembering a skill such as driving a car or learning a language) is less of an issue and so will not be discussed.

If you find you keep forgetting elements that you might think are procedural, eg infrequently used computer shortcuts, the issue you have is that the skill is not learned enough to become a true procedural memory, and so it is still fact based but not practised enough. Procedural memory is pretty sturdy and isn't subject to the normal issues of memory but the material has to be well learned in the first place. Keep repeating your computer shortcuts to transfer the knowledge to procedural memory.

EPISODIC MEMORY

> *Memory is the diary that we carry about with us*　**Oscar Wilde**

Episodic memory is 'knowing that…' related to experiences personal to you. It includes all memories relating to you and your life; your autobiographical memory.

Think about a work scenario where failure of episodic memory may cause a significant problem – any instances of forgetting information personal to you. For example, do you forget times and places for appointments, do you open a blank email and forget who you are sending it to or are you asked by your boss for your opinion of a recent meeting and struggle to remember anything about it? These are all failures of episodic memory that may lead to mild embarrassment, or more significant work-related concerns such as looking unprofessional, uncaring or inefficient.

What time is your first appointment at work tomorrow morning?

When was the last time you gave 360 feedback to a colleague?

Did you attend that conference last year or the year before?

SEMANTIC MEMORY

Semantic memory is 'knowing that...' related to *general* knowledge. It includes all the factual based information you learnt at school and all the knowledge that you have developed during your working life.

Now think about a work scenario where failure of semantic memory may cause a significant problem – any instances where forgetting general work-related information may be an issue. For example, do you forget the names of colleagues, the acronym of the latest scheme or system being devised or the latest budget predictions? These are all failures of semantic memory and don't worry, they are the most common memory concerns within a business environment.

What is your organisation's mission statement?

How well did product A or division B in your company perform last year?

What were the 10 key points from the last meeting or presentation you attended?

STORAGE IN STM

NEED CONVINCING?

In STM the material we are trying to remember is stored based either on its sound or, if that is not possible (eg if you are trying to hold in your head a complex diagram or picture), in a visual format.

TASK

On the next page are four lists of words. Spend 30 seconds rehearsing a list, (make sure you cover the other lists so that you don't get distracted), then immediately write down on a blank sheet of paper as many of the words as you can remember in the order that you see them. Take at least a 10 minute break and then move on to the next list.

Copy your results into the table on page 36.

STORAGE IN STM

LIST 1	LIST 2	LIST 3	LIST 4
LAD	GOD	HUGE	ROAD
MAN	PEN	BROAD	HOT
TIP	RIG	GIANT	SAND
MAD	DAY	LOFTY	PENCIL
CAP	BAR	LARGE	LATE
CAN	SUP	HIGH	WALLPAPER
MOP	JOG	EXPANSVE	SCREEN
TAN	WAR	MASSIVE	OLD
TAD	BIT	MAMMOTH	GLASS
CAD	SET	GIGANTIC	YELLOW
TOP	CUT	VAST	FISH
LAP	PIN	TITANIC	SIREN

To avoid distraction, make sure you cover three of the lists so that only the one you are currently learning is visible.

STORAGE IN STM

	LIST 1	LIST 2	LIST 3	LIST 4
Number of words correctly recalled				

	LIST 1	LIST 2	LIST 3	LIST 4
Number of words recalled that did not occur in the list (intrusions)				

STORAGE IN STM

As STM stores information based on **sound**, there is often confusion when trying to recall information that sounds the same. List 1 contained words with similar sounds, while List 2 contained words that were similar in length but sounded different. List 3 had words with a similar meaning; List 4's words were of a similar length to List 3 but with different meanings.

If you completed the task, you probably found the sound based List 1 hardest, as the words are easily confused with each other. You may have remembered as many words as on the other lists but your mistakes (eg adding words that weren't on the list or confusing items that were on the list) will have been related to the sound rather than the meaning. For example, you may have put Map and Tap on your list. They are not on the original list but share a similar sound. I doubt, though, that you have falsely remembered words that share a similar meaning (eg brush instead of mop or brown instead of tan).

Meaning is irrelevant in STM so the items in List 3 will not have been confused in the same way (though you may have taken a guess and just generated a few words with a similar meaning!). List 3 should have been easier than List 1, but no different from List 2 or List 4.

STORAGE IN STM

To recap, **meaning is irrelevant** for STM. Information is stored based not on meaning, but on the auditory properties.

How can you use this to help you improve your STM performance? Strategies should not include anything that makes the material more meaningful. Not only is meaning unimportant, but trying to make the material more meaningful takes time and effort – time you don't have. If you are trying to remember something that is written, for example, you cannot help but process the meaning, but you should not consciously use a mnemonic or other strategy (such as those discussed later in the book).

Don't forget you have approximately 15 seconds in STM to 'use it or lose it'! See the section Improving Short Term Memory for effective STM strategies.

MEANINGFUL MEMORY

It is when you want to store information in LTM that the material you are trying to retain is often coded according to its **meaning**.

Long-term memories are stored in the brain by a connection or network of neurons. The connections are made based on the meaning of the material. The more strongly related the memories are in terms of meaning, the stronger the connection between neurons – recall one memory and a whole range of related memories are triggered in your brain. So, more importantly, if you forget a memory, you have a range of related memories that can act as physiological triggers to the forgotten information.

How exactly do the neurons 'decide' which other neurons to connect to during learning? It is thought that a protein called CREB is used to 'decide' which memories are strongly related to the new material, with eligible neurons being selected to join the memory network based on their CREB activity during learning (see diagram overleaf).

MEANINGFUL MEMORY

Latest sales figures down 10% this quarter compared with 12 months ago (NEW MATERIAL)

Sales figures for last year

Bob rang with meeting time tomorrow

Sales figures for last two years

Redundancy in sales department

MEANINGFUL MEMORY

The thick lines represent the strongest connections between the separate memories. These connections are the most meaningful; remembering one is likely to act as a cue to recalling one or all of the others. The thinner lines represent a connection with less strength, while the memory without any connecting lines is not meaningfully related to the memory 'network'. Recalling information about Bob's telephone call is highly unlikely to act as a cue to recalling other memories in the network.

MEANINGFUL MEMORY

 Did you know that emotionally-charged events are easier to remember not necessarily because of the personal meaningfulness of the material but because of the physiological effects of the flood of emotion?

STORAGE IN LTM
NEED CONVINCING?

TASK

Repeat the four word tasks on page 35, but rather than recalling the words immediately, rehearse one of the lists for 30 seconds then wait for **one hour** before writing, on a blank sheet of paper, as many of the words as you can remember.

Take at least a 10 minute break before starting the next list, remembering to leave one hour between the 30 seconds of exposure to the words and recall.

Copy your results into the table on the next page.

STORAGE IN LTM

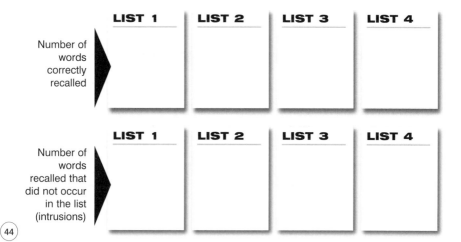

	LIST 1	LIST 2	LIST 3	LIST 4
Number of words correctly recalled				

	LIST 1	LIST 2	LIST 3	LIST 4
Number of words recalled that did not occur in the list (intrusions)				

STORAGE IN LTM

LTM stores information based on meaning, so confusion occurs when trying to recall words that share a similar meaning.

As sound is not relevant in LTM, individuals stop making sound-based errors once a task becomes an LTM task. Performance in List 1 this time should have been very different from when you did it as an STM task – I expect you made far fewer sound-based errors.

Not only is memory performance poorer in LTM when there is confusion over the meaning, you are also more likely falsely to remember words (intrusions) that share a similar meaning to those that did appear in the list.

For example, if you completed the task for list 3, did you write down TALL and BIG? Neither of these words appeared in the list but all of the words shared a similar meaning to them. It is easy to see from this how errors in LTM can occur; how you can turn up at 10 am for a meeting in the wrong room, one in which you had a meeting last week (related location), or report last year's sales figures in a presentation instead of this year's figures (related data).

STORAGE IN LTM

For LTM, meaning is everything. The most effective strategies to improve performance in LTM focus on the meaning of the material, but this must be meaning that is meaningful to **you**.

Just as memory is individual, so is meaning. It is also important to remember (pardon the pun!) that confusions can occur in LTM and this is a natural function of the way information is stored. There is nothing wrong (putting aside a little embarrassment) with making a confusion error, but by practising some of the LTM strategies and focusing on making the material you want to remember distinct from similar information, these errors can be reduced.

See the section Long-Term Storage Strategies for how focusing on making material meaningful improves LTM storage.

MEMORY PROCESSES

As well as the distinction between STM and LTM, memory can also be divided into three separate stages, or processes, all of which have properties and functions. By understanding how these processes work you can create a tailored effective memory strategy for the way your memory works at each stage:

Encoding

Encoding processes involve taking information from the world and transforming it into a form that the brain can store and that the memory can use. Knowing that in STM information is usually sound-based, while in LTM meaning is all-important, allows you to ensure that when trying to remember something in STM you ignore meaning and in LTM you focus on it.

Storage

Storage processes are required to ensure the material is retained in memory. Mnemonics are one way of improving memory storage (see page 90 onwards).

Retrieval

Retrieval processes involve remembering; getting the information out of memory. There are a number of strategies that can be used to improve retrieval (see page 109 onwards).

MEMORY PROCESSES

It is at the last of the three stages, retrieval, when people claim to have 'forgotten' information. Forgetting can occur as a result of a breakdown at any of the stages, however, and so the most effective way of using your memory is to ensure it is:

- **Encoded** appropriately
- **Stored** effectively
- **Retrieved**, using a technique if necessary

So, how can we do this? This is what the rest of the book is about.

Improving Short-Term Memory

REHEARSAL SPEED

As discussed, the amount of information you can store in your STM is determined by STM time and by output speed (how quickly you recall the information).

One very simple technique to improve the amount you can store in STM is to increase the speed at which you rehearse the information (whether the rehearsal is silently in your head or out loud) and the speed at which you output the information (eg write it down).

If you speak slowly when rehearsing the material and then output the information slowly, you may only be able to rehearse four or five facts or figures in the 15 seconds you have in STM.

By increasing the speed, you may be able to increase your STM capacity to more than nine pieces of information. In technical terms, increasing your **articulation rate** (the speed at which you speak) and your **output rate** (the speed at which you record the information you are recalling) can help improve the amount of information you can store in STM.

REHEARSAL SPEED

 Did you know that a consumer study demonstrated that as a result of 'tape loop' restriction in STM, every extra syllable in a product's price decreases its chances of being remembered by 20%?

REHEARSAL SPEED

Research into STM and articulation rate has consistently demonstrated a number of findings:

- Individuals who rehearse information more slowly have poorer STM than those who rehearse the information at a faster speed

- Changes in the STM memory of children are related to changes in their articulation rate; the amount they can remember in STM increases as they get older (corresponding with increases in their speaking speed – test this out with a 5-year old and a 10-year old)

- Nations with a generally faster articulation rate (eg Mandarin speakers) have greater STM spans than nations with slower articulation rates for the same material (eg Welsh speakers)

GROUPING

Say out loud your own phone number. Now do it again but listen to how you say each digit. Does each digit come one after another in a monotone way

(0...1...7...2...5...6...3...9...9...1)

or are they grouped in some way? In other words, do you cluster digits together to form small groups (0172...563...991)?

A second way to improve STM performance is to **group** the information when you rehearse it in your head (or out loud).

GROUPING
NEED CONVINCING?

In the section Structure & Types of Memory you may have completed the task (nine pieces of paper, each with a digit on it) which gave you a score for how much you could remember in STM.

How many digits did you remember? If you remembered all nine digits, do the task again but this time try 15 digits (closer to the length of a mobile phone number). How many can you remember now?

Complete the nine digit task again following the same instructions, but rather than turning over the pieces of paper at a rate of one per second, turn three over in quick succession, wait for four seconds, then turn the next three over, wait another four seconds and then turn over the final three. (Use this same method even if you are getting really ambitious and trying 15 digits or even 20 digits!) As you turn over each group of three rehearse the items together (so if you are using nine digits, the first three items will be rehearsed as a group, the next three as a group and the final three as a group).

GROUPING

Research has consistently shown that if you are trying to remember numbers or words in STM (perhaps long enough to add a phone number to your PDA, or sales figures to your report), the simple method of rehearsing the items in **groups of three** can considerably improve how much information you can hold.

Grouping is a very effective method of improving STM performance and it is a strategy you almost certainly were already using but may not have been aware of (did you group your phone number?).

Now that you are aware of it as a method, you can improve your STM from perhaps eight or nine pieces of information to around 20 with just a little practice. So, next time you are on the phone and don't have a piece of paper to hand, try using the grouping strategy to keep all the information in your head long enough to jot it down.

LONG-TERM STORAGE STRATEGIES

MEANINGFUL MEMORY

Earlier we looked at the importance of meaning in LTM.

There is a vast array of strategies that can be used to help improve the storage of information in LTM, some of which will be covered in this section.

All of the most effective methods have one basic premise – **make the information meaningful to make the information memorable**. But remember, the most effective way of improving your memory is not just about making the material meaningful, it is about making the material meaningful to you!

THE IMPORTANCE OF MEANING
NEED CONVINCING?

Make a list of all the types of information that you most frequently forget at work (eg phone numbers, appointments, names). Next to the list, rate each item for meaningfulness, that is, how meaningful the information is to you. Use a scale of 1 – 5, with 1 being not at all meaningful (eg the phone number of a colleague you rarely speak to) and 5 being highly meaningful (eg the name of your boss).

If you review the list, the majority of forgettable items are likely to have been rated as 1 or 2, that is, the material you most frequently forget is that which is less meaningful to you (or you care least about).

The key message is that the meaning is only pertinent to **you**. Some people can remember all the FA Cup winners from the last 20 years. Others would find that almost impossible but know the birthdays of all their friends. Often individuals who are thought to have exceptional or 'photographic' memory are just very well practised at using a mnemonic strategy, based on making meaningless information more meaningful to them.

CHUNKING FOR MEANING

Before considering the range of more complex mnemonic strategies that can be used to help an individual create meaning and therefore improve LTM storage, it is worth highlighting the fact that the best memory techniques can be very simple and yet very effective.

Look at the random string of digits below for 20 seconds and then, on a blank piece of paper, write down as many of the digits as you can remember, in the order that they were presented (and this time don't try to **group** them – that is a great strategy but is 'cheating' in this task!).

1066196910191473

CHUNKING FOR MEANING

Now look again at the digits and try to create meaning by 'chunking' the numbers into meaningful clusters. For example:

1066 refers to the Battle of Hastings

1969 is the date of the first moon landing

10 Downing Street is the address of the British Prime Minister

1914 was the year that the First World War began

7 refers to the number of dwarfs in the Snow White fairy tale

3 refers to the number of bears in the Goldilocks fairy tale

Of course you will find it easier if you can create meaning personal to you, such as the birthday or house number of a close friend, your extension number at work or some of the digits from your PIN number (the more personal the connection, the more effective the strategy will be).

CHUNKING FOR MEANING

The key is to take random numbers and chunk them in a meaningful way.

Now test your memory again for the sequence of numbers. How many can you now remember?

When could you use this strategy in a business environment? How many times do you need to remember strings of random numbers? Probably more often than you think – phone numbers, alarm and door codes, PIN numbers, sales figures, budget predictions and birthdays of colleagues (a fantastic skill for increasing your personal impact and networking ability) to name but a few.

Of course, you could try the STM grouping strategy introduced earlier. In grouping you do not create any meaning with the information, you merely 'group' the items together. In chunking you are creating **meaning**. Grouping would work but don't forget, it is only effective in STM. You may need to remember your pin number or work door code for longer than 15 seconds!

CHUNKING FOR MEANING

 Did you know that even when doing ordinary tasks such as washing the dishes or making the bed, the brain automatically chunks these continuous events into smaller segments?

LONG-TERM STORAGE STRATEGIES

CHUNKING AS A STRATEGY

Nobel Prize winner Herbert Simon with a colleague, William Chase, examined the memory performance of a group of expert chess players (Grand Masters) compared with a group of novice chess players.

Chase and Simon found that when the chess board was arranged in a meaningful pattern (eg halfway though a game), the experts were able accurately to remember the position of each piece on the board, whereas novices were only able to remember the positions of approximately seven pieces (similar to the amount of random information you can retain in STM).

If the chess board was 'rearranged', however, so that all the pieces were placed in a random position on the board, the memory performance of experts and novices was identical; on average both groups remembered the location of seven items.

CHUNKING AS A STRATEGY

Chase and Simon found that when the board was in a meaningful composition the experts were able to use their knowledge, create meaningful links or 'chunks' between individual pieces and therefore remember more items (eg they could chunk three chess pieces together if that formed a particular move, thus reducing three sets of information to one chunk).

Novices were unable to draw on any experience of chess, failed to create any meaning and were, therefore, unable to chunk pieces together to improve memory performance. The difference in memory performance between expert and novice chess players can be explained by how meaningful the material was to the individual.

Chunking differs from STM grouping because it forces you to create meaning. Grouping in STM is purely a matter of spatial organisation (remember that STM relies on sound not meaning).

MEANINGFUL CATEGORIES

 Did you know that a form of chunking occurs naturally in children as young as 14 months?

In an experiment, 14-month old children were shown four toys which were then hidden in a box. The children were allowed to search the box for the toys, not knowing that sometimes two of the toys <u>had not</u> been put in the box. Researchers found that the children, having retrieved two toys, continued to look for others. This occurred more often when the four toys were two groups of two very familiar items, such as cats and cars, and when one cat and one car were the two items withheld from the box.

CHUNKING AS A STRATEGY

In a business environment you have a wealth of skill and knowledge at your finger tips. Use this information to 'chunk' material you want to learn, as it will allow you to remember more.

For example, if you are creating cue cards for an upcoming presentation, chunk the topics into meaningful clusters. Rather than having 25 different topics (and therefore 25 different cue cards) can you organise them in some way?

Imagine you are a medical rep, about to present to a group of doctors the vast amount of medical information relating to a new drug your company has just taken to market. Scenario A on the next page sets out a typical list of topics. Rather than scenario A, try scenario B. The same information is included but scenario B has clustered the information into units that are meaningful for a medical rep with industry knowledge.

CHUNKING AS A STRATEGY

Scenario A

1 Introduce self.

2 Introduce company.

3 Discuss recent sales success of company.

4 Introduce new drug.

5 Compare new drug with current drug on market re placebo effect.

6 Compare new drug with current drug on market re double-blind trials.

7 Compare new drug with current drug on market re other studies.

8 Compare new drug with current drug on market for short-term cost (more expensive than current drug on market).

9 Compare new drug with current drug on market for long-term benefits (greater efficiency therefore fewer referrals back to doctor).

10 Compare new drug with current drug on market for side effects.

11 Obtain order from doctor.

CHUNKING AS A STRATEGY

Scenario B

1 | **Introductions**: self, company, drug (Cards 1-4 Scenario A)

2 | **Performance comparison** with current drug on market: placebo effects, double-blind trials, other studies, side effects (Cards 5-7 and 10 Scenario A)

3 | **Cost/benefit comparison** with current drug on market: (Cards 8-9 Scenario A)

Someone with industry knowledge will know the sort of detail a doctor needs to hear in order to decide whether or not to purchase a new drug. There is no need to over-complicate. The cues group the topics together to provide security that nothing important is forgotten. And there is no card required for the final step (obtain order) – would any sales person need a cue to remind them to go for a sale at the end of a meeting?

Often, when we are trying to remember information by using notes or cue cards, we include too much information. You need to trust your knowledge. You are an expert in your own domain and your knowledge will guide your memory.

ATTENTION & EFFORT
NEED CONVINCING?

While creating meaning is the key to successful memory storage in LTM, this creation of meaning takes **attention**, **effort** and **motivation**. You need to care about the information, or at least care about wanting to *remember* the information.

TASK

Consider the list you have created of information you most frequently forget. If you didn't do this, go back to page 59 and complete the short task there. Examine the list again, this time scoring each item for how much effort and/or attention you give to trying to remember each item. Score on a scale of 1 – 5, with 1 relating to no effort/attention and 5 indicating significant levels of both.

It is highly likely that there is a correlation between the scores you gave for meaning and the scores you have subsequently given for effort/attention; ie, the items that were most forgettable (or hardest to remember in the first place) are those that lack meaning **and** those where you exerted little attention and effort in trying to remember.

ATTENTION & EFFORT

When individuals in a business environment complain about poor memory, the issue is not necessarily lack of sleep, or stress or any underlying physiological issue affecting their memory; it is because ultimately **they do not put in the necessary time or energy to remember the material**.

This is not complex scientific theory – if you don't pay attention to the material and don't try to remember it, you **won't** remember it. Be honest with yourself. How often at work do you blame 'poor' memory when actually you have not made any real attempt to remember the information?

ATTENTION & EFFORT

*❝ The true art
of memory
is the art
of attention ❞*

Samuel Johnson

LONG-TERM STORAGE STRATEGIES

ATTENTION & EFFORT

Often, when individuals claim they have a poor memory it is actually a self-fulfilling prophecy – 'I am not going to be able to remember everybody's name at this meeting, therefore I will not waste my time and effort in trying.'

Creating meaning with, to you, meaningless material is a highly successful memory strategy but it takes attention and effort. Whenever you feel you are in a situation where memory storage failure may be an issue, consider the following questions:

1. Am I really paying attention to the material?
2. Am I sufficiently motivated to make the effort to remember? Do I care about this?
3. Am I creating meaning (for me) out of this material?

Without answering **yes** to the first two questions you will be unlikely to succeed at the third.

MNEMONIC CONSIDERATIONS

Mnemonics (a method or system for improving memory), once practised, can greatly improve your memory for a huge range of material. However, there are several limitations to the usefulness of the more complex mnemonics within a busy business environment, and often following the simple premise introduced earlier (make it meaningful to make it memorable) is enough to improve memory performance to the level required.

In addition to the chunking technique previously mentioned, more straightforward ways of improving LTM storage are covered in the rest of this chapter (which, in an environment with time constraints, you may find the most useful) before the traditional and more labour-intensive mnemonics are briefly introduced.

LONG-TERM STORAGE STRATEGIES

SKILLED MEMORY

Chase and Ericsson (the same Chase who worked with Herbert Simon on the study of chess players) proposed in 1982 a theory of skilled memory (what we all aim for!) in which they stated that there are three strategies to successful memory ability:

- **Meaningful encoding** – achieved by relating the items to the person's knowledge (making the information meaningful to you)

- **Structured retrieval** – achieved by adding cues to the items for use during retrieval (eg thinking about where you are or who you are with when you learn the material)

- **Practice** – enables the processing to become less effortful and more rapid

A number of simple techniques to improve LTM storage, focus on the first of these ideas – meaningful encoding. More complex mnemonics use all three of these principles.

MEANINGFUL ENCODING – ELABORATIVE PROCESSING

Meaningful encoding means that you relate the item you wish to remember to something that you already know. One of the best ways to encourage you to use your own prior knowledge when trying to retain new information is to ask yourself the question 'Why?'.

Think beyond the new facts being presented to you and consider *why* it makes sense.

Rather than being a passive recipient of the information (the sitting back and 'make me learn' attitude often demonstrated within school environments and all too common in the workplace!), try to relate the information you are learning to knowledge that you already hold.

MEANINGFUL ENCODING – ELABORATIVE PROCESSING

Ask yourself the following questions:

- How is this related to what I know about the topic?
- Why is this information new?
- Do I disagree with what I am learning? (Intellectual disagreement can be a great memory mechanism; it shows you have engaged with the material and have related it to information already stored in your memory, therefore making meaningful connections)
- How does this new knowledge fit with what I already know?

These types of questions encourage active processing of the material and allow storage of the new information by making connections to existing knowledge.

Elaborative processing is a great tool for remembering presentations, on training courses, when reading reports and when listening in meetings – any situation where a large amount of information is delivered and you have the opportunity to think about what the material actually *means* to you.

MEANINGFUL ENCODING – PRIOR KNOWLEDGE

Relating new material to previously stored knowledge is a very simple, yet effective technique for improving memory.

On the following page is a paragraph taken from a CEO's speech, discussing a change strategy being introduced into the company in the next few weeks. Read the paragraph on the following page **once** and then close the book.

Try and recall as much information as you can remember from what you have read.

MEANINGFUL ENCODING – PRIOR KNOWLEDGE

The procedure is actually quite simple. First you arrange items into different groups. Of course one pile may be sufficient depending on how much there is to do. If you have to go somewhere else due to lack of facilities that is the next step, otherwise you are pretty well set. It is important not to overdo things. That is, it is better to do too few things at once than too many. In the short run this may not seem important but complications can easily arise. A mistake can be expensive as well. At first the whole procedure will seem complicated. Soon, however, it will become just another facet of life. It is difficult to foresee any end to the necessity for this task in the immediate future, but then, one can never tell. After the procedure is completed one arranges the materials into different groups again. Then they can be put into their appropriate places. Eventually they will be used once more and the whole cycle will have to be repeated. However, this is a part of life.

Taken from Bransford, J.D. and Johnson, M.K. (1972). Contextual Prerequisites for Understanding some Investigations of Comprehension and Recall. Journal of Verbal Learning and Verbal Behavior, 11(6), 717-726.

MEANINGFUL ENCODING – PRIOR KNOWLEDGE

- How much information did you remember?
- How much of the information you have listed is related to change strategies?
- How confident are you that the information you have remembered appeared in the text?

Now go back to the previous page and re-read the text, but this time consider the paragraph to be a description of 'Doing the Washing'. How much information can you now recall?

Once you have a small amount of information, or a context (such as the title), then storing information in memory is significantly easier. An ambiguous paragraph (and it certainly was ambiguous!) becomes less so and you can draw on previous knowledge (of doing the washing) to help you store the current material.

MEANINGFUL ENCODING – SCHEMA

How does this relate to memory in a business environment? Access to the title 'Doing the Washing' allows the brain to use a 'washing day' schema; that is, a set of knowledge and information about the world relating to washing.

Using a schema allows you to draw on your own previously stored knowledge to help learn new material. Connections are made in the brain between memories, determined by meaningful relationships between the information. By thinking of one idea/thought/memory, the brain activates a series of other related memories. So, thinking about a schema activates a whole range of memories, allowing you to remember a wealth of information.

You will have schemas for a variety of work topics; either personal (your office and department schemas) or more generic (schema about the new marketing plans or the new CEO). By activating the relevant one you will access a range of memories, any one of which may be what you are searching for. Unfortunately, relying on a schema also makes it possible to remember 'false positives', information that fits but was not actually present in the material. You may well have remembered some change-related information from the earlier text, when you thought it was a speech on change.

MEANINGFUL ENCODING – SCHEMA

 Did you know that in a study, adults did better at remembering pictures of imaginary animals than they did remembering pictures of real cats?

Their prior knowledge of cats allowed the adults to generate a schema of cats, so they categorised the information but ignored individual details.

MEANINGFUL ENCODING – ORGANISATION

Previously we talked about the importance of using your own knowledge to group or chunk items, therefore reducing the memory load and allowing you to remember more.

Chunking the information, as shown in the example of the expert chess players, is a form of organising the material. Organising the to-be-learned material to aid memory is an easy strategy to adopt, yet is extremely effective.

MEANINGFUL ENCODING – ORGANISATION

NEED CONVINCING?

On the following page is a list of words. Read the words for one minute and then, on a blank piece of paper, write down as many of the words as you can remember, in **any** order.

MEANINGFUL ENCODING – ORGANISATION

Cow	Giraffe	Goat
Blueberry	Tiger	Strawberry
Pig	Rhino	Apricot
Kiwi	Banana	Duck
Hen	Melon	Raspberry
Apple	Orange	Nectarine
Bull	Grapefruit	Plum
Goose	Monkey	Lion
Donkey	Sheep	Satsuma
Peach	Grape	Horse

MEANINGFUL ENCODING – ORGANISATION

Compare your list of words with the list presented on the previous page. Have you listed the words in clusters according to whether they are animals or fruit? Perhaps you have even categorised the types of fruit, eg put all the berries together.

Even though the information to be remembered was presented in a random order, the brain prefers to organise the material according to meaning and previous knowledge, and this is reflected in the way you have recalled the information.

This spontaneous grouping or clustering of items has been studied by psychologists for many years and suggests a very simple way to improve memory storage. If the information to be remembered is not presented in a meaningful or logical manner then manipulate or re-arrange the material to create structure or organisation, drawing on your previous knowledge of the material to do this. You can organise **any** material into groups that are meaningful for you.

PRACTICE – DISTRIBUTED PRACTICE

The third strategy, noted by Chase and Ericsson, was practice. (The second strategy, retrieval, forms the subject of the next chapter.)

When trying to learn a motor skill (driving a car, operating a piece of machinery), research has shown that distributed practice, where a short break is included between each practice session, leads to faster and better skill development than if no breaks occurred.

When learning verbal material (such as material for a presentation, or names of key contacts at a conference), a scenario much more likely in a business environment, there is no difference between massed (all at once) and distributed (with breaks) practice in the **rate of learning** (that is, getting the information into the system in the first place).

However, and this is crucial, there **is** a difference in the **rate of forgetting**, particularly when the gap between learning the information and using the information is longer than 24 hours.

PRACTICE – DISTRIBUTED PRACTICE

Distributed practice leads to significantly longer retention of material than massed practice. In general, it rarely matters how quickly we learn the material; the critical factor is **whether we can remember it when we need to**, so distributed practice is the key.

This means that when you are learning new material (eg slides for a presentation) that you need to remember for longer than a day, distributed practice should be used. Cramming, or massed practice, will only allow you to remember the material for up to 24 hours.

Eg, if you are learning material on Monday for a presentation on Friday, try dividing two hours of learning time into four 30-minute sessions over a period of at least two days, with repetition of the material at least once per day. During the intervals it is important to avoid any tasks that may interfere with the material being learned.

LONG-TERM STORAGE STRATEGIES

PRACTICE

DANGER OF MASSED PRACTICE

Massed practice, or cramming, will allow you to maintain the information in your head for 24 hours at most. (Do you recall doing final exams at university and remembering the information for precisely the three hours of the exam and then promptly forgetting everything?)

The important consideration here, however, is to 'maintain'. You will be able to maintain or rehearse the information in your memory in a verbatim (or parrot) fashion, that may be sufficient if you are to deliver a monologue without interruption, such as a speech. Unfortunately, the delivery of this information will often be stilted, appearing false or inauthentic, and you will literally be 'reading' from your memory; there will be no demonstration of understanding the material and if you are interrupted, lose your flow or answer questions, you are likely to lose the memory.

In addition, memory based on massed practice is very susceptible to nerves – the more nervous you are, the less likely it is that you will recall the information learned this way. Distributed practice allows longer retention, encourages understanding and is, therefore, less fragile memory when you are interrupted, nervous or bombarded with questions.

COMPLEX MNEMONICS

Mnemonics are not tricks; they are devices to improve memory. They make use of the key memory principle of meaningfulness, while also creating associations between the material to be remembered and an easy-to-remember frame of reference. They also ensure that attention is maintained.

There is a vast range of mnemonics that require practice before use, and the effectiveness of each method will rely on individual preferences, the time you have available (some more complex mnemonics take considerable time to master) and the material you wish to remember.

We will look at three strategies that cover all the basic principles common to every complex mnemonic and are effective for material common to the business environment:

- The memory journey ('loci' mnemonics)
- The number shape system and number rhyme system ('peg' systems)
- The visual imagery method and the social method for names and faces

THE MEMORY JOURNEY

The memory journey technique is a loci mnemonic; a method of 'placing' each item to be remembered in a specific location within a journey well-known to you. The method can be used with any journey; the important principle is that it must be well-known (or 'over-learned'); a journey that can be recalled with little effort. Examples for you could include your journey to work, to school, to the local shops or even a journey around a house.

The only other central aspect to consider is that the journey must have at least 10 'stops' or landmarks that, again, can be remembered with little effort, and *in order*.

This method is particularly useful when you need to remember information in a specific order, for example key points for a presentation, or the names of people sitting around a meeting table. Once you have your list of landmarks, the task is to visualise each piece of information and mentally place each one, in the relevant order, at each landmark.

As the landmarks are concrete, rather than abstract, they are easy to visualise and as they form part of the 'over-learned' journey the order is naturally easy to recall, thus requiring little cognitive effort.

MEMORY JOURNEY EXAMPLE

A journey to work passes the following 10 landmarks:

Postbox

Local supermarket

Duck pond

School

Wooded area

Fire station

Large roundabout

Swimming pool

Hospital

Car park

The list of information to be recalled (cues for tasks to be completed that working day) includes:

Email

Questionnaire for HR dept

Report

Team meeting

Phone

Calculator

CEO

Printer

USB pen

Computer

MEMORY JOURNEY EXAMPLE

To use the method, you now need mentally to travel the journey to work and 'place' each item (**as a strong visual image**) at each location. So you would visualise the pile of emails as resting on top of the postbox, the questionnaire to be completed as so large that it blocks the entrance to the local supermarket, etc).

Once you have placed all the items at the appropriate locations using visual imagery, to recall them you simply mentally revisit these destinations, in order, and 'see' the item to be remembered.

THE MEMORY JOURNEY – PRACTICE
NEED CONVINCING?

Think about a journey that is very familiar to you; it needs to include at least 10 landmarks that you can recall, in order, with ease.

Place each of the items listed earlier (or create your own list) at a location in your journey. You may find it easier to do this by closing your eyes and creating the visual image, or you can draw a map of your journey and sketch a representation of each piece of information at the appropriate place. Both these methods are equally effective but you shouldn't need to take any more than five minutes to complete the task.

Now take a blank piece of paper and list all 10 pieces of information in the order that you recalled them.

As this mnemonic aids LTM storage you will still be able to recall the information after a delay in time, so try waiting for an hour and then repeat the recall of the items.

THE MEMORY JOURNEY – MULTIPLE LISTS

The memory journey mnemonic is very efficient in terms of time taken to learn, and is an excellent way of remembering anything that needs to be recalled in a specific order. If more than one list of information is being learnt, or needs to be recalled, at the same or similar time, however, it is advisable to use a second journey to reduce interference and confusion between the lists.

Now you have practised the method, you should be able to use the same principle to remember significantly longer lists and much more abstract information, such as the key points for a presentation: increased budget, office relocation, new team member, etc.

PEG SYSTEMS

The peg system is a mnemonic based on the same principles as the memory journey but using a mental hook (or peg) on which to hang the items to be remembered.

As with the memory journey, peg systems allow lists of items to be remembered and recalled in order; this is done through associations with the numbers 1 – 10 to indicate order.

The mental hooks are concrete words that are learned prior to using the mnemonic. For this reason, the peg system, while highly effective, can take a considerable amount of time to master, as a lengthy list of words must first be 'over-learned'.

VISUAL & RHYMING PEG SYSTEMS

There are two well-known peg techniques and the preference will be determined by your learning style (do you prefer to learn information that is presented visually, eg diagrams, pictures and mind maps, or do you prefer the written or spoken word?).

The visual system uses peg words that *look* like the numbers 1 – 10 while the other utilises peg words that *rhyme* with the numbers 1 – 10.

VISUAL & RHYMING PEG SYSTEMS

Number	Visual System	Rhyming System
1	Candlestick	Bun
2	Swan	Shoe
3	Heart	Tree
4	Yacht	Door
5	Hook	Hive
6	Elephant's Trunk	Sticks
7	Axe	Heaven
8	Egg Timer	Gate
9	Tennis Racket	Wine
10	Bat and Ball	Hen

PEG SYSTEMS – EXAMPLE

Once you have learned the 10 peg words so well that any number automatically brings to mind the desired image, or rhyme, then the list of items to be remembered can be 'pegged' upon each word by creating a strong visual image. For example, using the visual peg system, if a list of cue words for a presentation included...

- Team structure
- Finances
- New team member

...the first item could be stored by a visual image of the team seated around a large dining table lit with candlesticks (1 is represented by a candlestick and the item to be remembered is team structure), the second image could be a swan with a budget report in its mouth, the third image the new team member with a comic over-sized heart pounding in his or her chest.

Recalling the information involves thinking of each number, which should automatically allow recall of its peg word, which then relates to the stored visual image combining the peg word and the relevant item.

LONG-TERM STORAGE STRATEGIES

PEG SYSTEMS – PRACTICE

NEED CONVINCING?

Which of the two peg systems just described do you intuitively prefer, the visual or the rhyming method? Spend some time learning your chosen peg words and then try using the system to recall, in order, a list of items you need to remember.

As with the memory journey technique, the peg system is a strategy for improving LTM storage, so try to recall the items after an hour, after two hours and after a day.

These systems are complex and take significant time to learn. Deciding whether it is worth investing the time will largely depend on how much you need to learn (the systems can work with huge numbers of items) and how often you will need to remember such vast amounts of information. But they do work – most of the World Memory Champions of the past 10 years use this type of strategy, although they practise for several hours a day! In 2007, David Farrow remembered 59 packs of 52 cards in order (3068 cards) with one error (nobody is perfect) using a mnemonic technique.

For more information, eg numbers up to 20, go to http://www.memory-improvement-tips.com/remembering-lists. The best method, however, is to create your **own** peg list first. It will be more effective and easier to remember if it is meaningful to you.

MEMORY FOR NAMES

When individuals are asked to think about an aspect of business where the memory load is at its highest (trying to remember the most new information in the quickest time) and memory failings are most common, the favourite response is 'remembering the names of people during networking events'.

As LTM is stored most effectively when the information is meaningful, it is not surprising that people struggle to remember the names of people they have just met for the first time. These names are likely to be abstract and meaningless to you.
Also, in networking situations the speed of input is often particularly fast (being introduced to a large number of people at the same time or in quick succession) so there is little opportunity to try and create meaning before the next person is introduced.

101

LONG-TERM STORAGE STRATEGIES

FACIAL RECOGNITION
NEED CONVINCING?

As facial-recognition computers, we are actually very efficient. People are normally very good at recognising whether an individual is familiar or unfamiliar, but the difficulty arises when individuals are then required to give a name or provide other personal information.

TASK

Take a copy of a newspaper and cut out the photographs of 20 individuals you do not recognise (avoid famous people). Separate the 20 photographs into two random piles, and place one pile (face down) in front of you.

Turn each photograph from this pile over (at a rate of one every four seconds) and study the face before turning over the next cutting. Then mix up all 20 images and turn each one over (one every four seconds) and separate them into two new piles, those facial you remember having seen previously and those that are new.

You may be surprised by your accuracy at recognising familiar faces. I expect you made decisions based on 'just knowing' you had seen the face previously. I doubt you remember much detail though!

LONG-TERM STORAGE STRATEGIES

FACIAL RECOGNITION

People are generally excellent at facial recognition and require only a very short period of time to view a face before being able to make familiarity judgements.

If you find it difficult to remember the names of new people, try to focus your effort on remembering the **information** being presented to you (name and personal details) rather than on the person's facial features, as recognition of the face will happen almost automatically and will be easier than remembering the, to you, 'meaningless' verbal information.

With names, the difficulty is in trying to remember a relatively ambiguous piece of information (particularly surnames) and then match that information to the face. The strategy on the following pages will help.

PUTTING NAMES TO FACES

Look and see
Sharpened observations of your surroundings
will connect you to the moment of the meeting
and therefore, strengthen your memory, and
provide additional recall cues (see also
Cognitive Interview section).

Listen carefully
Attention is a key element in memory, and
in a situation where you may be nervous
or bored, attention often wavers.

PUTTING NAMES TO FACES

Practise active listening
It is common in networking situations to be ready with standard questions (*'What do you do for a living?'*, *'Do you have any children?'* etc). This discourages you from actually listening to the other person and then generating a question based on their response.

Enter the event without pre-prepared questions, focus on listening to the other person and create meaning (for **you**) out of what they say. For example, *'Oh, you have three children. I only have one child. I don't think I could cope with three, but **my sister** has three and I do admire her'* or *'Wow, you must be busy if you work in accounts and then sail at the weekend. I love sailing but **I can't say** I love doing my accounts!'*

PUTTING NAMES TO FACES

Repeat the name out loud
Repetition is important in memory (see below) but repeating the name also checks for correct pronunciation (it is often difficult to 'unlearn' a name that has been incorrectly learned).

Write the name down
If at all possible, reduce the cognitive and memory load, and write the name down (no, that isn't cheating!).

Use the name throughout
The more often you repeat the name, the more likely you are to remember it, so use it during greeting and during departure as a minimum.

PUTTING NAMES TO FACES

Use association and/or imagery to remember the name
If you find generating visual images a relatively effortless task (a visual learner?), creating a visual image **related to a name** often aids the storage process. For example, does the individual look like somebody famous, or is there a specific aspect of their face that is striking that you could focus on and create a strong image from (glasses, moustaches and noses are favourites). It helps if the visual image is exaggerated and/or humorous and you have to link it in your mind to the person's name.

If you are a verbal learner, and find creating images difficult or time-consuming, then don't waste time on this technique – you are likely to spend so much time focusing on creating a visual image that you will fail to remember anything!

PUTTING NAMES TO FACES

Ask about personal history/exchange information
The more information about the individual you can elicit, the more likely you are to find material that you can use to create a meaningful connection, and the more cues you will be able to draw on at the retrieval stage (see next section on retrieval strategies).

Check your memory
Engage in a checking process at intervals throughout the meeting (either in your head or out loud through the conversation) to ensure the key information is being stored.

LONG-TERM RETRIEVAL STRATEGIES

THE COGNITIVE INTERVIEW

Even if material has been stored effectively, using a mnemonic technique or other method of creating meaning, you can still fail to remember this information when trying to recall it. This failure is the point at which a person claims to be demonstrating forgetting.

Many methods can be used to improve access to previously stored information, ie material you know you 'have in your head' but just cannot retrieve. The combination of these techniques is called the *Cognitive Interview* and is frequently used by trained police officers to improve the accuracy of witness and victim statements after a crime.

Imagine a situation you might be involved with:
You have been asked to summarise the key recommendations of an important meeting, write a brief report, and present the recommendations to your team. During the meeting you were listening and involved in the dialogue and did not, therefore, take any notes. When you sit down to write the report you realise you remember very little of the detail.

Now read the four stages of the Cognitive Interview on the following pages, and consider how you could use the strategies to help you recall the information from the meeting.

THE COGNITIVE INTERVIEW

STAGE 1: REINSTATE THE CONTEXT

If you are struggling to recall a piece of information (whether it is a budget figure for a financial report or the name of the Chair of the last meeting you attended) try to **reinstate the context**.

It helps if you are physically able to do this (eg return to the room where the meeting was held), but often it is sufficient just to create a visual image of the situation you were in when you learnt the material.

Consider the physical surroundings, the smells and the temperature. Reinstating the emotional context is as important as the physical context, so consider the mood you were in, how you were feeling and how others were feeling at the time. The effectiveness of context reinstatement to elicit 'forgotten' memories is the reason that crime reconstructions are used.

THE COGNITIVE INTERVIEW

STAGE 2: VARY TEMPORAL ORDER

When people recall events in the order in which they occurred, they often reconstruct what is likely to have happened rather than what actually happened. If, for example, you have mislaid your office keys, and retrace your steps in order, from when you entered the building to where you are now, you are more likely to retrace your 'typical' route than the one you actually took on this occasion.

By working backwards, any gaps or assumptions are highlighted and information you had previously ignored or failed to consider is often shown to be key in helping reclaim the memory. Recalling information backwards is also cognitively more effortful, so more concentration is required, more attention is paid to the forgotten material, and therefore success in recall is more likely.

To recover the missing information from your meeting, start at the last item on the agenda and work backwards.

THE COGNITIVE INTERVIEW
STAGE 3: CHANGE PERSPECTIVE

When trying to recall information, people often think about one particular viewpoint and have one specific perspective.

In the same way that recalling backwards highlights presumptions, changing your perspective highlights a narrow focus and interpretation which may prevent information from being remembered.

Try choosing a different perspective to help retrieve the information you have forgotten from the meeting, for example that of a colleague from a different department.

THE COGNITIVE INTERVIEW

STAGE 4: RECALL EVERYTHING

Now recall everything you can think of that is vaguely connected to the material you have forgotten, no matter how irrelevant you think this may be.

Memory stores information by making connections in the brain between pieces of related material, so recalling a piece of information can often trigger another memory, that in turn triggers another one. This chain reaction often leads to the 'forgotten' material relatively quickly.

Use the principle of recalling everything that happened in the meeting as your final strategy to help retrieve the forgotten information.

SCENARIO SOLUTIONS

Context

Return to the room where the meeting took place.

Sit in the chair you took during the meeting.

Consider how you were feeling and the mood of the room during the meeting.

Order

Start by considering the closing statements by the Chair of the meeting.

Work backwards through the meeting, thinking last about when you walked in and sat down.

Perspective

Try and recall the meeting from the viewpoint of the Chair, considering what would have been pertinent to them.

Change perspective and now consider the viewpoint of the person taking the minutes.

Everything

Note down everything you can remember from the meeting, trying not to focus on what you think is important.

What colour shoes were you wearing, how hot was the room, how quickly did the Chair move through the agenda?

LEARNING TO COPE

A useful acronym to help you remember this series of techniques is **COPE**.

To help you **COPE** with memory failure remember:

C ontext

O rder

P erspective

E verything

COGNITIVE INTERVIEW RESEARCH

Why does the Cognitive Interview work? It is based on memory research that demonstrates the effectiveness of each technique.

1: Context

The Encoding Specificity Principle is a psychological concept that notes that you will remember more when the memory cues available at the encoding stage (when you see or hear the material for the first time) are the same as, or as close as possible to, the cues at retrieval (when you are trying to recall the information).

Reinstating the context maximises the chance of the cue being similar, if not identical.

Research has shown that even when the context is extreme (learning words in a diving suit at the bottom of a swimming pool), physically reinstating this context improves memory recall.

COGNITIVE INTERVIEW RESEARCH

2: Order

The research reveals that more information is recalled if individuals recall first in a forward order, followed by a reverse order, than if two forward order recalls are used.

3: Perspective

Research conducted by psychologists found that when 'house buyers' were asked to recall as much information about a house as they could, changing their perspective to a 'house burglar' allowed them to produce a number of other pieces of description about the house that they had previously forgotten.

4: Everything

By recalling everything, research has shown that alternative retrieval cues can be used to access previously forgotten material.

For example, the location of a budget meeting to be held next week in London may be accessed through the cues of budget/finance/payments/profit & loss but equally may be accessed through city/head office/theatre/tube.

USING MIND MAPS

A technique that can be used to help with Stage 4 of the Cognitive Interview: Recall Everything, is the construction of a mind map. Create a mind map, placing the information that has been forgotten as the central 'bubble'. Add in absolutely everything you can think of around this central bubble. This strategy mirrors the way that LTM is stored in the brain.

Got 'blue' in the title

About increased visibility

Name of the project the Marketing Department are about to launch?

Brief given by CEO

John is leading the project

Brief given in Leeds

Brief given last week

Simone is writing the copy

THE FOUR W's

Another method to aid retrieval if you find you are struggling to recall information is to use the four W's:

 Who? **When?** **Where?** **Why?**

By using these questions as a series of retrieval cues you should be able to reach the information you are searching for. For example, if you are trying to recall four action points from a meeting you recently attended, ask yourself:

- **Who** was at the meeting?
- **Who** was asked to action each of the points raised?
- **When** was the meeting?
- **When** were each of the action points to be completed by?
- **Where** did the meeting take place?
- **Why** was the meeting held?

LAST THOUGHTS

SYNESTHESIA & EIDETIC IMAGERY

Individuals who demonstrate exceptional memory are very rare; the memory feats shown on television or demonstrated at world memory championships are performed by people using mnemonics. They practise for many hours a day and their impressive memory skills are purely a demonstration of their ability to master the technique.

One of the few documented cases of exceptional memory was a Russian named V.S. Shereshevskii (known as 'S'), studied by the psychologist Luria in the 1960s. S could remember vast arrays of digits (100 x 100 grids) and, as long as there was a pause between each item of roughly 3-4 seconds, retained the information indefinitely (yes, he never forgot it!). S was found to demonstrate synesthesia; a condition where hearing a sound stimulates other senses. S saw lights and colours, with each digit that he heard corresponding to a unique pattern of light and colour, thus providing more cues for recall.

S was also found to use eidetic imagery, commonly known as a photographic memory. Eidetic images are more vivid and detailed than regular visual images. They last significantly longer and allow the individual literally to 'read off' the information from the after-image.

THE FORGETTING CURVE

How quickly we forget was initially studied in 1885 by a German psychologist called Hermann Ebbinghaus. Ebbinghaus was interested in how quickly information is forgotten in memory and so, using himself as the participant in a study, he examined how quickly he forgot nonsense syllables (such as TOV, BOJ). The results of his lengthy experiment provided the basis for the forgetting curve shown on the next page, which indicates the approximate time taken to forget relatively meaningless information if it is not revisited (ie if there is no practice or attempt to rehearse the information).

Half the information you learn is lost within the first 20 minutes, two thirds within two days and 80% within a month. While forgetting is advantageous (as demonstrated by the mental illness of the unfortunate S) and allows you to negotiate the world around you in an effective way, the forgetting curve is an important piece of research as it indicates how quickly meaningless information is lost.

The key points to consider are that information is less likely to be forgotten if it is meaningful to **you**, and if it is revisited (or practised).

THE FORGETTING CURVE

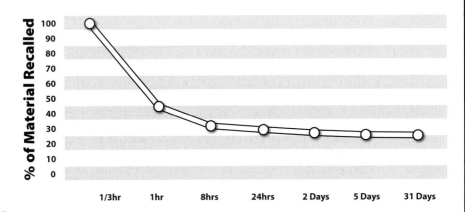

LAST THOUGHTS

YOUR AMAZING MEMORY

At the end of a Pocketbook on memory it is very tempting to leave the final page blank and ask you to fill it in with what you remember!

I hope that you are now in a position to understand a little more about how your amazing memory works (and if you think about everything it can do, it really is amazing). You now know the excuses you can use (poor sleep and stress), and the one that you can't (ageing), and have a variety of tools and techniques up your sleeve to help improve both your STM and LTM.

I will leave you with a final thought: **every time you revisit (or recall) a memory, you create a new memory trace in your brain, so every memory is unique and is not the same as the memory of the same fact or event last time you remembered it**.

Memory is deceptive because it is coloured by today's events.

Einstein

THE MANAGEMENT POCKETBOOK SERIES

Pocketbooks (also available in e-book format)

360 Degree Feedback
Absence Management
Appraisals
Assertiveness
Balance Sheet
Business Planning
Business Writing
Call Centre Customer Care
Career Transition
Coaching
Communicator's
Competencies
Creative Manager's
C.R.M.
Cross-cultural Business
Customer Service
Decision-making
Delegation
Developing People
Diversity
Emotional Intelligence
Employment Law
Empowerment
Energy and Well-being
Facilitator's
Feedback

Flexible Workplace
Handling Complaints
Icebreakers
Impact & Presence
Improving Efficiency
Improving Profitability
Induction
Influencing
International Trade
Interviewer's
I.T. Trainer's
Key Account Manager's
Leadership
Learner's
Management Models
Manager's
Managing Assessment Centres
Managing Budgets
Managing Cashflow
Managing Change
Managing Customer Service
Managing Difficult Participants
Managing Recruitment
Managing Upwards
Managing Your Appraisal
Marketing

Meetings
Memory
Mentoring
Motivation
Negotiator's
Networking
NLP
Nurturing Innovation
Openers & Closers
People Manager's
Performance Management
Personal Success
Positive Mental Attitude
Presentations
Problem Behaviour
Problem Solving
Project Management
Psychometric Testing
Resolving Conflict
Reward
Sales Excellence
Salesperson's
Self-managed Development
Starting In Management
Strategy
Stress

Succeeding at Interviews
Tackling Difficult Conversations
Talent Management
Teambuilding Activities
Teamworking
Telephone Skills
Telesales
Thinker's
Time Management
Trainer Standards
Trainer's
Training Evaluation
Training Needs Analysis
Virtual Teams
Vocal Skills
Working Relationships
Workplace Politics

Pocketfiles

Trainer's Blue Pocketfile of
Ready-to-use Activities

Trainer's Green Pocketfile of
Ready-to-use Activities

Trainer's Red Pocketfile of
Ready-to-use Activities

18.03.10

About the Author

Dr. Vicki Culpin, PhD, MPhil, MSc, BA (Hons), CPsychol, AFBPsS, AFHEA

Vicki is the Ashridge Research Director and a member of the Ashridge faculty. She works with a range of clients, nationally and internationally, from the public, private and cultural sectors and delivers guest lectures around the UK on a variety of psychological topics.

Vicki specialises in memory, sleep, research methodology and statistics. She has spent over 14 years researching memory, the impact of poor memory, how to improve memory and the effects of reduced sleep.

She delivers workshops on a wide range of psychological issues including memory and leadership, the impact of sleep on decision-making and simulations around decision-making and heuristics. She also works with clients designing and analysing psychometric tools and surveys and supports other Ashridge faculty on the design, implementation and analysis of their research (including multivariate statistics).

Vicki studied Psychology at Manchester University, followed by an MPhil and PhD in Psychology from Lancaster University and an MSc in Applied Forensic Psychology from Leicester University. She is an Associate Fellow of the British Psychological Society, a Chartered Psychologist and a Fellow of the Higher Education Academy.

ORDER FORM

Your details

Name _____

Position _____

Company _____

Address _____

_____

_____

Telephone _____

Fax _____

E-mail _____

VAT No. (EC companies) _____

Your Order Ref _____

Please send me:

No. copies

The Memory _____ Pocketbook ☐

The _____ Pocketbook ☐

The _____ Pocketbook ☐

The _____ Pocketbook ☐

Order by Post
MANAGEMENT
POCKETBOOKS LTD
LAUREL HOUSE, STATION APPROACH,
ALRESFORD, HAMPSHIRE SO24 9JH UK
Order by Phone, Fax or Internet
Telephone: +44 (0)1962 735573
Facsimile: +44 (0)1962 733637
E-mail: sales@pocketbook.co.uk
Web: www.pocketbook.co.uk

Customers in USA should contact:
Management Pocketbooks
2427 Bond Street, University Park, IL 60466
Telephone: 866 620 6944   Facsimile: 708 534 7803
E-mail: mp.orders@ware-pak.com
Web: www.managementpocketbooks.com